YOUR KNOWLEDGE HAS VALUE

Mohamed Rahama

Data Structures and Algorithms

GRIN Publishing

Imprint:

Copyright © 2012 GRIN Verlag GmbH
Print and binding: Books on Demand GmbH, Norderstedt Germany
ISBN: 978-3-656-34658-6

This book at GRIN:

http://www.grin.com/en/e-book/204115/data-structures-and-algorithms

GRIN - Your knowledge has value

Since its foundation in 1998, GRIN has specialized in publishing academic texts by students, college teachers and other academics as e-book and printed book. The website www.grin.com is an ideal platform for presenting term papers, final papers, scientific essays, dissertations and specialist books.

Visit us on the internet:

http://www.grin.com/

http://www.facebook.com/grincom

http://www.twitter.com/grin_com

Atlantic International University

Second Phase Assignment

Data Structures and Algorithms

Student Name: Mohamed Ahmed Mohamed Osman Rahama

Table of Contents:

1. Introduction

Data are intended to the substantive facts sets and concepts, which we see and deal with it in our daily lives. Data and facts are the things that we do not feel there is a relation or knowledge, directly or indirectly with them. It is a set of values that reflect the entities or events expressed by, for example, book, car, university, institution, etc., are all independent entities and facts. Conversely, there are many facts that are difficult to cover and know all their fractions because of the multiplicity of their data and their characteristics, which leading to organize them in sets, arrays, strings, records, files and other patterns and so-called data structure. Data structure refers to a set of data elements that have a special organization, and also special style for accessing the individual elements, either through the process of storing or retrieving values. On the other hand, the data structure means the different ways and methods through which the logical perception of the data is interpreted as seen by the computer programmer who cares about the different ways to organize the data and developing algorithms to manipulate this data. · According to Lafore "A data structure is an arrangement of data in a computer's memory (or sometimes on a disk). Data structures include arrays, linked lists, stacks, binary trees, and hash tables, among others". The word structure is used in many areas to describe the large entities that have been built from small blocks in recursive way, and data structure is the logical block caused by repetitive data elements according to specific order and relations. Data structures is considered as the intermediate stage between the files on the storage media and the application programs

The algorithm is a set of well-defined rules to find the best solution to a problem in a limited number of steps, and to be so, the set of rules must be clear and have a distinct breaking point. Algorithms are the procedures or formulas to solve a problem and evolved with time closely linked with the programming of computers devices. Algorithms can be expressed in any language of natural languages such as Arabic, English, Spanish or French and using programming languages such as JAVA, C, Pascal, Delphi and C++ as examples. Algorithms were invented by an Arab mathematician named Muhammad Bin Musa Al-Khwarizmi and the word "algorithm" is referred to his name. Al-Khwarizmi lived as part of the royal court in Baghdad during the year 780 to 847, and he used algorithms in solving mathematical problems. The most of the computer applications, with the exception of some artificial intelligence ones consist of algorithms. The creation of elegant, compact, smart and simple algorithms that require fewer steps possible is one of the main challenges in computer programming. Data structures are objects generated to store data and algorithms are a set of instructions to perform specific task by using the data structures. As computer programmers we think algorithms are the lifeblood of our work and it is the nerve that gives the life to any computer program. In brief, we can define the data structures and algorithms in one statement as Sally and Kenneth says " the structural organization is known as a data structure, and the ways in which the operations are carried out are known as algorithms", (2008).

The objectives of this paper is concentrated in introducing the basics of data structures such as arrays, linked lists, trees, stacks, queues, and hash tables. It also incorporates data structures into the applications associated to them and determine which algorithm or data structure to use in different scenarios. Through this paper we will discuss and implement various searching and sorting algorithms such as linear search and binary search using java programming language.

2. Abstract Data Types (ADTs)

The organization of information is one the main issues for every software developer. The decision for software development is affected by conceptual and structural fundamentals. Conceptualizing information means the way we think for implementing the best and easy solution. The process of conceptualizing information is known as Abstract Data Type (ADT). Abstraction is the way for creating the model that defines the problem. Abstract data type ADT is the mathematical pattern comprises a structure for storing data and processes that can be performed on that data. ADT means the creation of a good definition for an entity to be properly handled. According to http://en.wikipedia.org ADT "is a mathematical model for a certain class of data structures that have similar behavior; or for certain data types of one or more programming languages that have similar semantics" [8]. ADT is characterized by a type and sets of operations called interface, and the interface is the mechanism for accessing the data structures. Common ADT includes sets, trees, stacks, queues and heaps. In computer programming environment, ADT is referred to a set of data specified by the programmer in terms of information that can be contained and processes that can be done with it. The data type is said to be "abstract" because of the sense that it is independent of various applications. Setting ADT is the first step in application design process because it provides the definition of application interface. In computer programming data types are defined through variables which contain numerical data when dealing with numbers, symbolic data when dealing with characters and words and logical data when dealing with data that bearing right or wrong. All of these data types are classified as simple data types. For example, int, byte, float, long, short, double, Boolean and char are the simplest data types used in java programming language. The simple data types are used to describe entities in records and tables which are called structured data types.

According to the above can be drawn benefit of using compositions abstraction that the programmer who is trying to use a combination of data abstraction this in the application software large and complex is the focus of his thought in the matter, which tries to programming solved without effort is in the details of the structure of the data, which makes the program more effective and less complicated and therefore easy in terms of writing logic, understanding and modification

3. Data structures

The way for structurally organizing the data in memory to achieve the high efficiency for carrying out operation on information is called data structure. Data structure is the physical implementation of ADT. For example, the data structure for customer entity may contains the customer ID, name, address, birth date, balance etc. Data structures are divided into several types each of which correspond to a special method in computer program design and electronic

3

processing and can be classified as the following three types: linear data structures, tree data structures and graphs data structures.

- The linear data structure is dealing with stacking data within the memory on a single line and these include: arrays, string, records, tables, lists, stack and queues.
- The tree data structure is concerned with the hierarchical data structures like the tree representation of data set for a large family or an organizational structure of a company.
- Graphics data structure is concerned with graphics and in other words, if any element of a lower level in the tree data structure linked with more than one element at a higher level is referred to by name data graphics structures.

3.1 Arrays

Arrays are defined as a set of similar elements, and these elements can be a numeric value, symbolic value, combinations of numeric value and string, or a set of records, and they are classified in terms of the dimensions into two classes: one dimensional array and multiple dimensional array.

For example, if the student scores in database systems, mathematics, operating systems, software engineering, Delphi language and data structure courses are 80, 75, 68, 90, 76, and 83 respectively, we can create an array of six elements to store these values as in Fig (1). The data for student scores are stored in array of six elements and their corresponding addresses started from 0 to 5. The values can be inserted or retrieved from arrays according to these addresses and in our example here if we named this array by *studScores* then we denote any of the array elements by the array name followed by the respective index such as *studScores(1)* to refer to mathematics and *studScores(5)* to refer to data structures course and so on. That means the *studScores* array is represented by *studScores[n]* where *n* is the index that referencing the array elements.

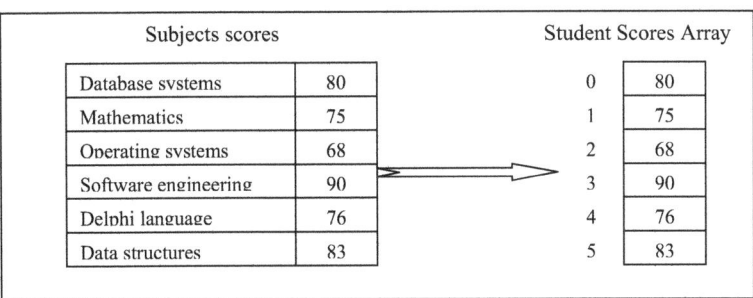

Fig (1) One dimensional array

Using java programming language we can define an array by issuing the following statement:

int[ ]   arr;   *// where arr is a reference to an array of integers*

4

The array can be defined and created physically on the computer memory when we issue the following statement:

int[ ] arr = new   int[20];   *// initialize an array of 20 elements*

and we can assign the value 200 to the third element and 100 to the last element of the array (arr) by using the following statement:

arr[2] = 200;   *// gives the array element no. 3 of index 2 the value 200*
arr[19] = 100;   *// gives the array element no. 20 of index 19 the value 100*

In our previous example we discussed how to represent the scores in six courses for one student in one-dimensional array, and if we decide to store the scores of database systems, mathematics, operating systems and software engineering for five students as shown in Table (1), we will need a tow-dimensional array to store their data.

Students	Databases systems	Mathematics	Operating systems	Software engineering
Ahmed	80	87	66	68
Ali	90	96	63	70
Omer	72	67	74	65
Hassan	55	87	56	76
Nadia	67	76	45	82

Table (1) Students scores

The array will consist of four columns and five rows, and if we named it stScores, then it will be referenced by *sts[m, n]*, where *m* is the index of rows and *n* is the index of columns and it is represented in memory as shown in Table (2).

	Databases systems	Mathematics	Operating systems	Software engineering
Ahmed	sts(1,1) 80	sts(1,2) 87	sts(1,3) 66	sts(1,4) 68
Ali	sts(2,1) 90	sts(2,2) 96	sts(2,3) 63	sts(2,4) 70
Omer	sts(3,1) 72	sts(3,2) 67	sts(3,3) 74	sts(3,4) 65
Hassan	sts(4,1) 55	sts(4,2) 87	sts(4,3) 56	sts(4,4) 76
Nadia	sts(5,1) 67	sts(5,2) 76	sts(5,3) 45	sts(5,4) 82

Table (2) The two dimensional array structure

The three-dimensional array is considered as a repetition of the two-dimensional array in more than one level and we can reference its items by adding the index of the level to be sts[m,n,k]. We can define the two-dimensional array above in java and assigning them values like that in the above example we can issue the following statements:

int[ ] [ ] sts = new   int[5] [4];   *// initialize an array of 5 rows and 4 columns.*
sts[5] [4] = 82;   *// gives element at row 5 column 4 score 82*
sts[1] [1] = 90;   *// gives element at row 1 column 1 score 90*

The main Characteristics of arrays can be summarized in the following points:

- It is found in all programming languages.
- It has the ability to deal with them directly and easily at any array position.
- It has contiguous positions making it easier to access them.

The disadvantages of arrays can be summarized as follows:

- Consist of a fixed size and is determined at the beginning when they are defined.
- Contain only one type of data elements.

3.2 Stacks

Stacks are more abstract data structure than arrays and any other data storage and their implementation mechanisms are not visible to users. Stack is a special container for temporarily storing data and accessing it through a specific mechanism. As Goodrich and Tamassia defined its purpose "A *stack* is a collection of objects that are inserted and removed according to the last-in first-out (LIFO) principle", (2006). Stacks allow accessing only one item at a time, the last item inserted is accessed first, or in other words the Last-In-First-Out (LIFO) mechanism and the item next to the last item can be accessed when removing the last item and so on. The stack is actually like the pistol, where the last bullet is fired first and when it is released, the bullet which followed become ready to be shot the next, and so on until we fired at last the first bullet inserted i.e. the insertion and deletion is doing at the highest by using pushing and popping functions respectively and the top pointer i.e. doing the top one first as shown in Fig (2). Stacks are used for temporary storage for addresses and data while the program is running.

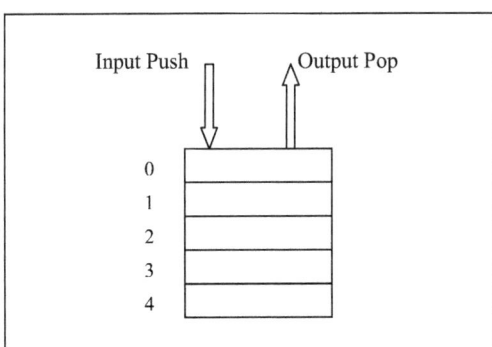

Fig (2) Stacks structures

The most benefits of using stacks are represented in finding the values of arithmetic expressions, using for the recursion purposes and calling of sub-programs. The pointer top holds the index value -1 when the stack is empty and this value is incremented by one whenever a new value is inserted in the stack until filled. During the out process the stack pointer value is decremented by one until its value becomes -1 which indicate that the stack is empty.

For example, suppose that we have the values a, b and c stored in stack and we need to store a new value d, and after that we decide to pull a value from the stack, it will be the last value entered The methods used for representing stack elements in memory with putting into account the ways for storing and retrieving values can be classified as in the two following points:

- Interconnected ring representation of stack elements in memory as a list.
- Compact representation of stack elements in memory in the form as a one-dimensional array.

In java programming language we define the stack in the same way that we define the one-dimensional array as in the following statement:

long[ ]   stackRef;   // where stackRef is a reference to stack long integer.
stackRef = new   long [10];   // initialize the stack of 10 elements

3.3 Queues

The queue Is a type of linear data structures and it resembles the stack in term of temporary storage of data while different from the organization that applied to input and output data while differ in the operation of input and output mechanism, the queue uses the First-In-First-Out FIFO mechanism. As Harris and Ross defined it, "a queue is a collection of objects that are inserted and removed according to the *first-in first-out (FIFO)* principle".

The queue has two pointers: head or front pointer and tail or rear pointer and the processes of insertion and deletion are done at the end and front of the queue respectively. The tail is incremented by one in the insertion process while the head is incremented by one in the deletion process. The data elements are organized sequentially and adjacent side by side like people when they stand in line to pay in the super market, the first one in the queue is served first. Queues are used in programming to model real world status.

There are two types of queues: linear queue and circular queue. The linear queue have a specific size and it becomes full when the value of the tail equal to the queue size. The circular queue characteristics is the same as linear queue but differ in its fullness condition, the circular queue, however, becomes full when the head is equal to one.

The linear queue becomes empty when the values of the head and tail are equal to -1 and this means that the queue pointers are not referring to any element. When the first value is inserted in the queue the head and tail pointers are incremented by one and their values become zero, and when the subsequent values are entered the tail pointer is incremented by one with any entered value while the tail pointer value remains as is. The deletion process is reverse to insertion process, where the tail remains constant while the head is incremented by one and one with any deletion process and all the remaining queue elements are shifted to fill the resulting empty cells caused by deletion.

The circular queue have advantage over the linear queue, when the circular queue becomes full it will start overwriting items from beginning so that most new items or data won't waste. It is also logical because it is assumed that if an item is useful it would have been fetched before queue get full and if it is still there and when queue has reached to it's capacity it means overwriting the older items which it will not be harm. The circular queue not physically formed a circle within memory but only the front and rear pointers are wrapped around. While the linear queue can not accept any more items when it becomes full and this situation will result in overflow error. There is a small problem facing the use of linear queues, a case of false fullness although there are many empty places and that happens when we are clearing all the elements except the last element in the queue at which the tail pointer points to the end of the queue, and achieving fullness condition, this problem was solved by using circular queues.

A practical example of the application of queue exist n a multitasking operating system environment, where multiple processes are sharing the CPU time, and only one process is running at a given CPU time while all the others processes are in sleeping state. The administration of the CPU time is held by the scheduler who keeps all current system processes in a queue with the priority of active process to be at the front of the queue. Another example is the printer spooler which keeps all printed documents in a queue.

3.4 Lists and linked lists

According to Simon Harris and James Ross "a list is an ordered collection of elements supporting random access to each element", (2006). Lists are a type of linear data structures which consist of nodes that are accessed sequentially, and differ from queues and stacks in that they can be accessed for insertion and deletion operation at any point of the list. Many operations can be done on the list such as adding new nodes, updating an existing node, remove nodes, and reports about the empty and full nodes. Linked lists consist of a group of cells that interconnected with each other through a link and each element is called a node. Any node consists of two fields, one field to store the data value and the other to hold the address of the next node. According to wikipedia.org a linked list is defined as "a data structure consisting of a group of nodes which together represent a sequence" [8]. Fig (3) shows the lists and linked lists representations.

Linked lists are classified into three types: singly linked lists, doubly linked lists and circular linked lists. Singly lined list stores the data sequentially and there are a pointer named **head** references the first element in the linked list and a pointer **tail** references the last element in the list, and each node have an address which points to the next following node and the last node points to null.

8

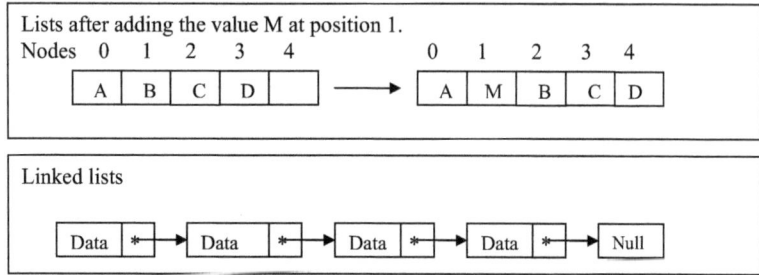

Lists after adding the value M at position 1.

Fig (3) Lists and linked lists representation

It is not necessary that the nodes to be arranged consecutively in memory and they relate with each other through the pointers. The singly linked lists are characterized by their ability to accept values at left or right or any position i.e. they allow the random access. When applying java programming to the singly linked list we can define the class Link which contains data and a reference to the next link in the list by using the following code:

```
class Link
{
        public   int      intData;    // data item
        public   double dblData;   // data item
        public   Link    next;         // reference to next link in list
}
```

In some singly linked list, the pointer of the last node can points to the first node i.e. the tail points to the head.

Doubly linked lists are actually singly linked lists but not vice versa. Doubly linked list have two pointers, the **next** pointer which points to the next node in the list while the other the **last** pointer points to the previous node. We use this type of list when we need to return back to retrieve specific data.as it happens in the word processing applications. Fig (4) illustrates the doubly linked list. Doubly linked list can be accessed for insertion and deletion operations in the same way as singly linked list.

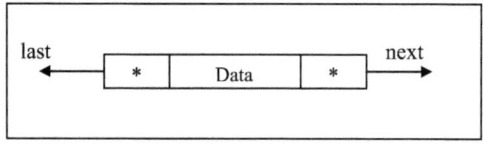

Fig (4) The doubly linked list structure

The main advantage of the linked lists is the ability to store a number of infinite data without having a predefined number like that in arrays and stacks.

3.5 trees

Trees are classified as a divergent and unordered data structures data type. Trees consist of root node, branches nodes and leaf nodes which are connected by edges. The first level content is called parent level and the next level content is called child or son level and each branch node is a root for sub-tree. The leaf nodes, however, have no son's nodes. In Fig (5) below the node A represent the root node, nodes B, C, and D represent the son nodes, and nodes E through L represent the leaf nodes. The most or major application of trees are records, groups, dictionaries and decision trees. Trees are considered as the better data structures and they are characterized by rapidly implementing special operations

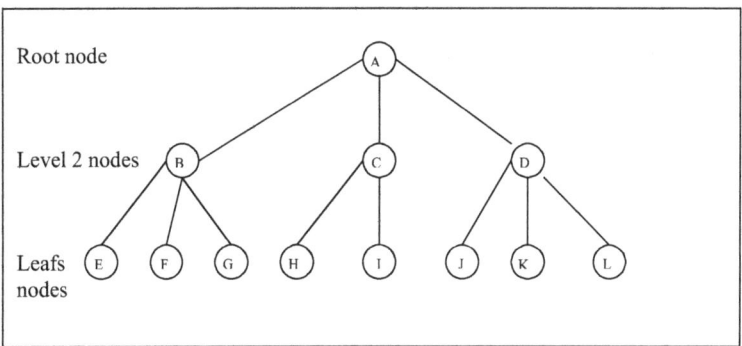

Fig (5) Normal tree structure representation

such as adding, removing, and searching elements and they are very fast compared to the other data structures. Trees are classified into many types: the common type is the binary tree; there are also balanced and red-black tree types.

The binary tree - see fig (6) - can be defined as the tree where each node containing two children at most, or in other words, each node must contains zero, one or two children only. The child can also establish a sub-tree, and therefore there could be two separate trees, called the left tree and the right tree, each of them is considered as a binary tree structures, and therefore the trees definition becomes recursive which facilitates the programming process. Binary tree structure is characterized by the presence of two pointers at most linked to any node, or in other words, a node can contain a single edge or two, or without edge and in this case is called a leaf. Traversing methods through trees intended to visit each node once and in a certain order for the specific purpose or action, and is mostly through three methods: in-order traversal, post-order traversal and pre-order traversal. In-order traversal is common and mostly used. In-order traversal method starts with the left child and its node, then to the right child and its node, and if the left or the right child or both contain a sub-tree, the left sub-tree is visited first and so on in recursive order. In post-order traversal method starts with left child and then right child and after that the node which we need its data. The pre-order traversal starts with the node which we are looking for its data, then the left child and the right child. The main characteristics of red-black trees are that the nodes are colored and the rules followed assure variety of arrangements of these colors.

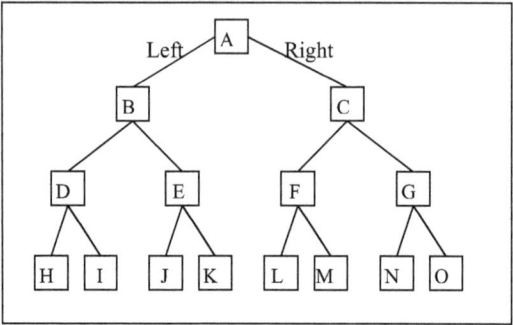

Fig (6) The binary tree structure

In order to define trees in java programming language we can design a class for the node and a separate class for the data that should be in the nodes. In the following example we take employee as a data class as in the following:

```
class Node
{
    int      intData;      // data used as key value
    double   dData;        // other data
    node     leftChild;    // this node's left child
    node     rightChild;   // this node's right child
}
```

3.6 Hash tables

Hashing is a mechanism used for storing relatively large amount of data in computer memory in a table called the hash table, with the possibility of implementing the following three basic operations within the hash table, insert, and the search, and delete. Hash tables are the fastest mechanism among the data structures and it is required in applications that are operating in interactive mode such as spelling checker. The need for hash tables comes because we need to do the prior operations in a short time, and in fact this is possible through direct addressing. The solution provided by the arrays and stacks is excellent when the number of data to be stored is small, but when the number of data becomes very large, it will drive us to choose a very large size of the array which will result in waste of a large area, and to avoid that we use hash tables and we use what so-called hash function. Fig (7) shows the hash table model.

For example, if we decide to store data for 200 students where their identification numbers (ID) are ranged between 0 and 2000, and if we assume that we want to record the ID numbers of students who chose a particular section in a particular college, in this case we have the selection of numbers between 0 and 2000, if we use direct accessing in this case, the only 200 IDs i.e. using the student ID as an index of the array, we will need an array consisting of 2000 cells, and there will be a 1800 empty cells. In order to solve this problem, we resort to the hashing mechanism and finding the array index by applying hashing function on student ID. By doing this we can store ID numbers in a table which is relatively small (200 or 300 cells). Thus, the space reserved is proportional to the number of keys (IDs) actually stored. The hash table has a load factor defined as the ratio of the data stored in the table to the length of the hash table and in this case it is 2/3 and that means a two-third of the hash table is used and if we use a hash table of 2000 cells it will be 200/2000 which is equal to 1/10 and that means one-tenth of the hash table is used and all the remaining is wasted.

Hash function is an arithmetic function and its input is the key of the element which we want to add to the hash table and its output the appropriate entry number of the hash table. The hash function should be characterized by the following:

- Be simple and calculated quickly, for example: the remainder of key over HashTableSize-1 (where HashTableSize is the length of the array).
- Distribute the keys equally over the hash table entries, to avoid collision as much as possible.
- The data being hashed determined its hash value.

The most disadvantages of hash tables are that they are depend on the arrays, and arrays are difficult to expand their size after they are created. There are some types of hash tables degraded the efficiency and performance when the table is become full, and therefore this situation requires the programmer to be careful and put a good idea to some extent to determine how many data elements are required for storage. Also the hash table's access mechanism is not convenience.

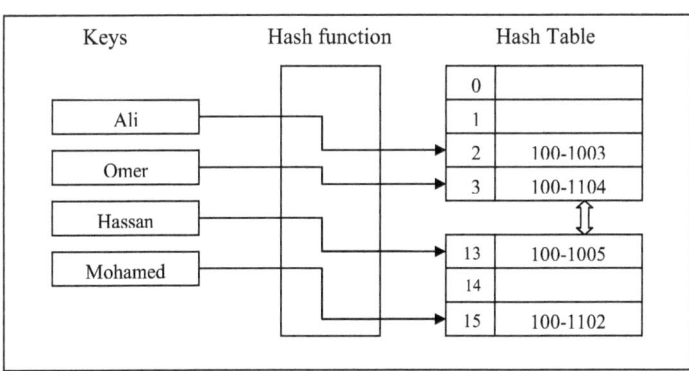

Fig (7) Hash table model

4. Algorithms

In our working life tends to be the values of variables are not arranged or sorted, by the way that the computer can be able to handle them perfectly. For example, we are mainly sorting the names alphabetically, or by age to lead the computer to do its role with high efficiency. While data structure deals with concepts and ways for storing data in computer memory, algorithms introduce the techniques such as inserting, searching, sorting, merging etc. for manipulating the data structures contents. For developing an algorithm we must know the formulation to resolve the problem by selecting the inputs, the output and determine the process steps for solving the problem, and the algorithms must be characterized by the following:

- Definiteness: every step of algorithm should have meanings, clear and unambiguous and must be understood of all people.
- Finiteness: all steps in the algorithm can be solved in a specific period of time.
- Effectiveness: Every step of the solution are possible and effective.

Any high level programming language is provided with an interpreter or compiler, the interpreter executes the program step by step directly in memory, while the compiler makes a compilation for the full program once on a disk file, and shows the results and errors. This means that the program is an algorithm and data structure. The software application program development goes through five stages: requirement specification, analysis, design, refinement and coding and verifications. Verification itself goes through three steps: proving, testing and debugging.

4.1 Algorithms analysis

Algorithm analysis is important for determining the efficiency and then it can be improved. There are two measures associated with the algorithms and its execution speed: the space complexity measure and time complexity measure. This means an algorithm that takes a long time to solve a problem is hardly of any use. Likewise, an algorithm that requires a very big space of computer memory can not be a useful.

Space complexity measure: memory space required for the program execution until its completion. This measure requires two segments: fixed segment and dynamic segment. The fixed segment is independent of the input and output characteristics and it includes the code space and the data space either it is simple or fixed complex variables The dynamic segment which is consists of the space which requires the program complex variables and depends on the size of the problem to be solved in addition to the stack space used in the reaction. The dynamic storage can be illustrated by the variables values that entered by the programmer who control them according to their names. The complex values are intended to elements of the stack where the pointer, programmatically and architecturally, is referred the top of the stack, and which concerns algorithms is the contents of the stack.

The time complexity measure means the amount of time required for the program development until to complete. Algorithm running time depends on many factors, such as computer hardware type, programming language, execution time, and the type of compiler or interpreter. Total execution time for an algorithm depends on the magnitude order of algorithm which means the total number of frequency counts for all execution statements under which the execution time is estimated for the algorithm. We must put into account whether the problem takes more than one case and focusing on the worst case of problems solution, because it may contains many complexities. We can also get rid of the difficulties in cases where statements selected is not appropriate or sufficient to determine the number of steps the algorithm, and this is achieved by specifying three types of steps: best case, worst case and average case for analysis. In order to understand the algorithm complexity we must run it in all possible situations, or either Skiena says "To understand the notions of the best, worst, and average-case complexity, think about running an algorithm over all possible instances of data that can be fed to it" (2008).

4.2 Algorithms performance measurement

Performance measurement is respect to the measurement of time on the computer and the its benefits thereof, and aims to get the real requirements of the program, in terms of storage and execution time, which depends on three factors: the computer hardware, programmer and the compiler. The algorithm runtime is the one which we must focus on it. In order to get the algorithm run-time it requires doing a test and planning for this test needs to put into account the following aspects:

- What is the precise time? and what is the accuracy of the results that we want? with the knowledge of the required results accuracy we can determine the length of the shortest event time measured.
- Determine the frequency factor and must be chosen so that the time of the event at least equal to the less time that can be measured with precisely desired. To measure the time a minor event it is necessary to repeat it several times and then calculate the average.
- What is the purpose of the test? Is it to compare the algorithms, or to predict its time? in the case of prediction we need to extend the event time by increasing the loop or occurrence frequency.
- Will measure the worst case or medium case? The test data generated is depending on the specific situation and there is no consistent strategy, and often relying on random values.

4.3 Searching algorithms

Searching in algorithm means the search for an item in a list through the surveying or reviewing the list items sequentially from beginning until we reach the item you want, if it exists, or accessing the to the end of the list in the case of not finding the item. There are many algorithms searching mechanisms such as linear search and binary search.

Linear search is the search for the value by means of the survey or review the list elements from the beginning sequentially until accessing the desired value in the case the list is sorted. If the list is not sorted requires a search in the all list until the desired value is found. In the case of accessing the list until the end without finding any results, this means the element is not within the list. In the case of looking for a value that exists in more than element in an unordered list, all elements of the list should be searched. To demonstrate the linear search technique we develop the SearchApp application shown in the program list below by using java programming language on an array of 100 elements as the data structure.

In this program we firstly create an array named arry of 100 elements. Then we create three variables nElements, j, and srchKey to refer to element number, loop counter and the key of the item which we are looking for respectively. The program then does the following steps:

1. Insert 10 values in the first 10 elements of the array.
2. Executes a (for loop) to display the values entered starting from the first value until reach last one.
3. Search for the value 69 in the array by mapping the value to array elements starting from the first one and break the search if the value exists. The value 69 existing in the forth element, and then the program executes the break statement with the value of the variable j equal to 3.
4. The (if) condition is then executed and return false because the value of j is not equal to nElements and the program display "Found 69".
5. The variable srchKey is assigned a value 08 to be deleted from the array, and when execute a search loop starting from first array element, the value 08 is found at the address 7 in element 8 and execute the break statement.
6. The value of the variable j counter is assigned to the k counter to be the start point for the next loop which shifts the reaming values existing in position 8 and 9 to position 7 and 8 respectively and fill the element at position 9 with null, this because we did not need an empty cell within the array.
7. Execute a (for loop) to display the items in the array starting from the first one until the last item and the output of this program is displayed as follows:

```
78 34 69 55 42 88 11 08 66 73
Found 69
78 34 69 55 42 88 11 66 73
```

```
// Algorithm to demonstrate linear search in Java arrays
// for running this program: C>java SearchApp
// -------------------------------------------------------------------------------
class SearchApp
{
        public static void main(String[ ] args)
        {
                long[]  arry;                      // array reference
                arry = new  long[100];             // create array of 100 elements
                int  nElements = 0;                // number of elements
                int  j;                            // counter for loop
                long srchKey;                      // search key for item
//-----------------------------------------------------------------------------
                arry[0] = 78;  arry[2] = 34;       // assign 10 items to array
                arry[1] = 69;  arry[3] = 55;
                arry[4] = 42;  arry[5] = 88;
                arry[6] = 11;  arry[7] = 08;
                arry[8] = 66;  arry[9] = 73;
                nElements = 10;                    // 10 elements in array
//-----------------------------------------------------------------------------
                for (j=0; j < nElements; j++)      // display items on screen
                        System.out.print(arry[j] + " ");
                        System.out.println("");
//-----------------------------------------------------------------------------
                srchKey = 69;                      // find item with key 69
                for (j = 0; j < nElements; j++)    // for each element,
                        if (arry[j] == srchKey)    // found item?
                                break;             // yes, exit before end
                if (j == nElems)                   // at the end?
                        System.out.println("Can't find " + srchKey);   // yes
                else
                        System.out.println("Found " + srchKey);        // no
//-----------------------------------------------------------------------------
                srchKey = 08;                      // delete item with key 55
                for (j = 0; j < nElements; j++)    // look for it
                if (arry[j] == srchKey)
                        break;
                for (int k = j; k < nElements-1; k++)  // move higher ones down
                        arry[k] = arry[k+1];
                        nElements--;               // decrement size by 1
//-----------------------------------------------------------------------------
                for (j=0; j<nElements; j++)        // display items
                        System.out.print( arry[j] + " ");
                        System.out.println("");
        }                                          //  main() method end
}                                                  //  class SearchApp end
```

List (1) Linear search on an array data structure

16

The binary search idea is to split the list into two parts and then excluding the part which does not belong to the key of the element we are looking for, by selecting the item which is located in the middle of this list or array, and then compare this element with the key and once again we exclude the half which is not related to the key, and so on till we reach the item which we are looking for. In binary search we can reach the item by doing a few guesses. One of the important issues concerning the binary search is that the list should be ordered.

Suppose that we are looking for the item of value 33 in an array or list ranged from 1 to 100. To find the number in the a few steps, we start by guessing the value 50 (divide by 2) and the value which we are looking for should either be high or low when compared to the required value. In this case the 50 is high when compared to the value 33, then we exclude the number ranged between 51 and 100, and this means that our value between 1 and 49. So in the next step we guess 25 and the answer should be low, and we exclude the number between 1 and 25, and this means that the value exist between 26 and 49. If in the next step we guess 37 which is high and result in excluding the number between 37 and 49. The value we are looking for now exists between 26 and 36. The next guess should be 31 which is low and results in excluding numbers between 26 and 31 and the new search range becomes between 32 and 36. If we guess 34 the result is high and we exclude the numbers between 34 and 36 and the number should be either 32 or 33. In the next step we can guess the number directly in one step or by two steps when 32 is guessed in stead of it.

Here we define a method named findItem() to demonstrate the binary search on the array data structure. The method is called from the main program with the parameter hold the key of the element which we are looking for, and the method executes as in the following steps:

1. Declare variables lowBound and uppBound of type integers to store the lowest and the highest boundaries of the array.
2. Declaring the variable curIn to store the result value of the division expression.
3. Executing the while loop and at the first statement divide the sum of lower limit and the upper limit of the search range by two and then check if the key provided in parameter srchKey is equal to the value resulted from the division.
4. If they are equal this means that the requested value is reached and the loop break by return statement which returns with the key of the item which we are looking for.
5. If they are not equal and the lowBound is become greater than uppBound then return with maximum array index which means the key is not exists among the array.
6. If the lowBound is become greater than uppBound then compare the result of division with the key which we are looking for.
7. If the key is greater than the value resulting from the division then we add one to the division result and assign the new value to the lower limit (lowBound) and execute the loop.
8. If the key is less than the value resulting from division then we subtract one from the division result and assign the new value to the upper limit (uppBound) and execute the loop.

17

```
public int findItem(long srchKey)
{
        int  lowBound = 0;                              // first element
        int  uppBound = nElements - 1;                  // last element
        int  curIn;                                     // storing division result
        while (true)
        {
                curIn = (lowBound + uppBound ) / 2;
                if (arr[curIn] == srchKey)       // arr is array in the caller program
                        return curIn;                   // item is found
                else if (lowBound > uppBound)
                        return nElements;               // item is not found
                else                                    // divide range
                {
                        if (arr[curIn] < srchKey)
                                lowBound = curIn + 1;   // it's in upper half
                        else
                                uppBound = curIn - 1;   // it's in lower half
                }                                       // else end
        }                                               // while end
}                                                       // method findItem() end
```

List (2) Binary search of an array data structure

4.4 Sorting algorithms

Sorting algorithm is the algorithm that organizes the elements in a data structure according to a specific order. The elements to be sorted are arranged in a group such as arrays, linked list, hash tables etc. relationship with a certain order arrangement· The classification of sorting algorithms is very important because it allows the algorithm to choose the most suitable type of processor taking into account the drawbacks that may be existing in the algorithm. In other words, the sorting is a process of arranging a set of data structure elements, according to a specific value called a field or group of fields called the key and the sorting is done in ascending or descending order. The main purposes of using sorting are:

• Increasing the algorithms efficiency.
• Simplifying the file processing because the files are composed of fields and sorting of these files by using keys ease the process of programming and searching techniques.
• Solving the problem of transaction similarities such as those occurring when names of customers, for example, become similar·

Sorting is classified into two types: internal sort and external sort. The internal sort happens within the computer memory in the case the volume of data is appropriate and not a large and includes selection sort, bubble sort, shell sort, insertion sort, radix sort, tree sort, topological sort and tree sort. External sort is the sort that happens in the auxiliary storage such as magnetic disks outside the computer memory. The external sorting is required when there is a large volume of data and it is difficult to accommodate data in memory during the sorting process, and external sort includes merge sort, balanced two way merge sort and divide and conquer merge sort.

The main factors required for selecting the sort algorithm are

- The volume of data stored: if the size is of small storage then an internal sort is used, but if it is of a large storage an external sort is used.
- Type of storage: If it is the main memory storage then it will be an internal sort, and if the storage is a magnetic disk it will be an external sort.
- The degree of order of the data: if the data is semi-ordered it will result sort is faster than the unordered data.

Selection sort algorithm is the most common, and is processed by searching for the largest component or the smaller one between the data structure elements and placed in the last place, then looks for the second largest or smallest element and put in place before the last, and so on until the entire table is arranged. For ascending order sort this can be illustrated through the following:

- Find the smallest item in the list and replace its position with the first item in the list.
- Find the smallest item of the remaining elements in the list and replace its position with the second item in the list.
- Continue this process until the last element is reached.

Fig (8) illustrates the selection sort algorithm; we notice that no action is taken in step 3 because the item is already in order.

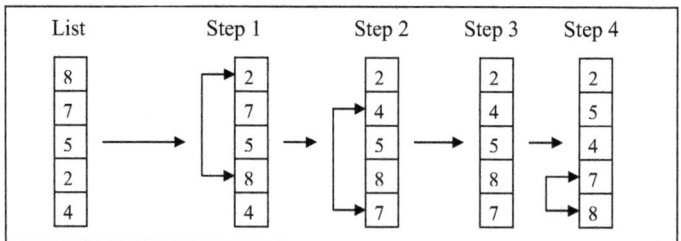

Fig (8) Selection sort algorithm

A bubble sort algorithm is criticized because it is slow. Bubble sort algorithm is working to raise the largest component as a bubble that rises to the top, by ordering the list elements in sequence, i.e. we compare the first and second elements and reserve the largest item, and we change places if they are not ordered. We do this process until we reach the last element, then re-operate the process to the pre-final place, and so forth. The bubble sort demonstration is shown in able (3) below

List	Step 1	Step 2	Step 3	Step4
8	8 8 8 2	2 2 2	2 2	2
3	3 3 2 8	8 8 3	3 3	3
9	9 2 3 3	3 3 8	8 7	7
7	2 9 9 9	7 7 7	7 8	8
2	7 7 7 7	9 9 9	9 9	9

Table (3) Bubble sort algorithm

Inserting sort algorithms is summarized in two points. The first one starts with the second element in the list and compares it with the first item, and we put it at the top of the list if the order was ascending. The second is to move to the third element in the list and compare it with the top of the list that containing the first and the second elements and put it in a second location, and the process continues until we get an ordered list. One of the disadvantages of bubbles is that the number of comparisons increases when the elements that must be in the first list are found far away from their order position in the list·

We notice that the inserting sort algorithm is reverse to the selection sort algorithm because it takes the item and compares it with the item which is just before it. In other words, inserting sort algorithm compares the first item with the second and the first with the third and so on. The table (4) shows how to steps for sorting an array consisting of seven elements.

List	Step1	Step 2	Step 3	Step 4	Step 5	Step 6
8	3	3	3	2	2	2
3	8	8	7	3	3	3
9	9	9	8	7	6	4
7	7	7	9	8	7	6
2	2	2	2	9	8	7
6	6	6	6	6	9	8
4	4	4	4	4	4	9

Table (4) The inserting sort algorithm

The shell sort algorithm Idea is based on dividing the list into virtual spaces called a gap, and making a comparison between two or more elements that are not adjacent but they are apart by the distance selected. Then we change their position if they are not ordered. The next step is to shorten the gap to the half and making comparison again, and so on, until the gap is become equal to 1, after that we change the position of the remaining items if they are not ordered until the list is sorted. Fig (9) illustrates the shell sort algorithm process. As shown in the figure the gap started with 4 and when it is became 1, the point at which the switching process is started until we got the sort. The shell sort algorithm is characterized by:

- The efficiency increases as the number of operations increases.
- There is no need for additional memory in order to make the sort.

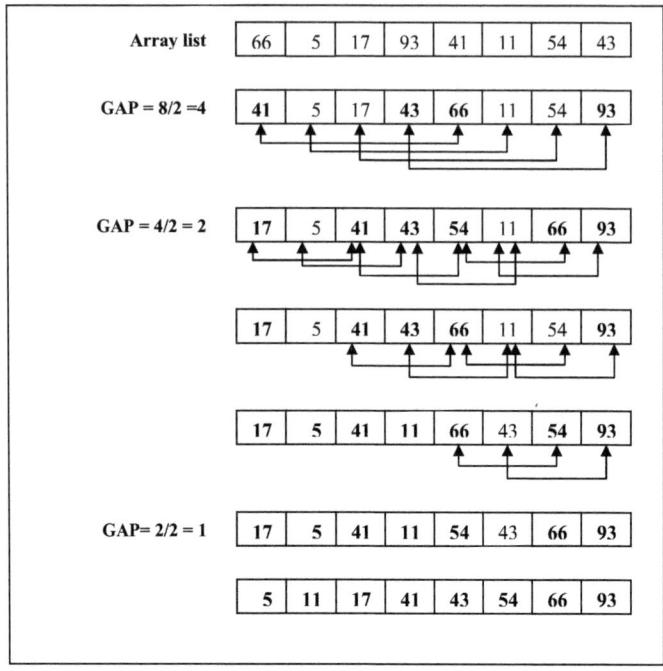

Fig (9) The shell sort algorithm

- Characterized by high efficiency if the processes within the list sorted or semi sorted.

The merge sort algorithm works on dividing the array gradually until each element become alone, and at the completion of the division, the process of integrating the elements is introduced. During the merge process, we combine the elements in order, and keeping the merging process gradually until the array is sorted. When the program starts the merging process begins by comparing the elements and takes the smaller and inserts it in the array and so on until the merge of all the elements is completed. The merge sort is one of the most fast and effective algorithm.

Topological sort algorithm uses this idea of the graphs and put the values in the queue. It is useful in areas that the data structure elements must be ordered in specific order.

4.5 Sorting algorithms examples in java

Java method code in List (3) shows a simple demonstration for the selection sort algorithm. The program starts by receiving the array x which we want to sort its element in ascending order. Then, a two for loops are executed and the first loop initializes the variable mIndex to store the index of the smallest

21

element. The next loop searches the array for the smallest item by comparing all array elements, and when the smallest item is reached, the loop exit with index. of the element containing the smallest item. Then, the next statement, the (if) condition is executed, and its purpose is to exchange the current item with smallest remaining items of the array. When the outer loop is finished the sort process is complete.

The java code in List (4) demonstrates the bubble sort algorithm. The program starts by creating an array and initializes it by values (5, 90, 15, 44, 35, and 30) according to the array index and then execute a (for) loop to display the array elements before the sorting process on the screen. Then the main program part call the method bubbleSrt() and pass to it the array elements. The method executes a nested for loop to sort the array according to bubble sort techniques.

```java
public static void selectionSrt(int[ ] sarr) {
    for (int i=0; i<sarr.length-1;  i++) {
        int  mIndx = i;              // Index of smallest remaining value.
        for (int j=i+1; j<sarr.length; j++) {
            if (sarr[mIndx] > sarr[j]) {
                mIndx = j;           // The value of new minimum index
            }
        }
        if (mIndx != i) {            // swap with smallest remaining.
            int tmp = sarr[i];
            sarr[i] = sarr[mIndx];
            sarr[mIndx] = temp;
        }
    }
}
```

List (3) Selection sort algorithm

```
public class BubbleSrt {
    public static void main(String[ ] args) {
        int intArry[] = new int[ ] {5, 90, 15, 44, 35, 30};      //create an int array
        System.out.println("Array before Bubble Sort");      //print before sorting
        for (int i=0; i < intArry.length; i++) {
            System.out.print(intArry[i] + " ");
        }
        bubbleSrt(intArry);                //sort an array using bubble sort algorithm
        System.out.println("");            //print array after sorting
        System.out.println("Array after Bubble Sort");
        for (int I=0; i < intArry.length; i++) {
            System.out.print(intArry[i] + " ");
        }
    }
    private static void bubbleSrt(int[] intArry) {
        int   n = intArry.length;
        int   tmp = 0;

        for (int i=0; i < n; i++){
            for (int j=1; j < (n-i); j++) {
                if (intArry[j-1] > intArry[j]) {   //swap the elements
                    tmp = intArry[j-1];
                    intArry[j-1] = intArry[j];
                    intArry[j] = tmp;
                }
            }
        }
    }
}
```

List (4) Bubble sort algorithm

After the sort is completed a (for) loop is executed to display the sorted array elements·

5. Recursion

Recursion is a function that makes call to itself until a certain condition is occur and stops running, then, is a way of loop such as for loop, but in a way the function call itself· Here, we would have a function with at least two conditions to be inside the function. The basic condition is when the loop is stopped or breaks and the second condition is to make calls to it. According to Simon Harris and James Ross recursion is defined as "a recursive algorithm involves a method or function calling itself" (2006). Recursion is technique applied for solving problem simply and effectively. The major advantages of using recursion can be summarized as in the following:

- The tasks that explore data structures that found in hierarchal design can easily use recursion algorithms.
- Recursion code is compact which makes the algorithm logic understandable and the very easy.

- Recursion reduces the size of the code to its minimum level which can not be found in any other programming techniques.
- Recursion helps in avoiding the redundant calling to the functions and procedures.

The main disadvantages of using recursion may be summarized as in the following:

- Using multiple recursion function may leads to confusion in understanding the program code.
- The recursive code sometimes becomes very difficult to trace.
- Sometimes recursive solutions require much more memory because during the call process it depends on the process control block, usually this is not considerable when the program is too small.

To demonstrate the recursion concept, let us discuss the famous puzzle tower of Hanoi as seen in Fig (10) below. As seen we have three towers A, B and C. The tower A contains three disks placed on each other in order and the smallest one on the top. The idea of the puzzle is to transfer the disks from tower A to tower C by using intermediate tower B. Only one disk should be moved at a time, and no disk of large size can be placed on a smaller disk.

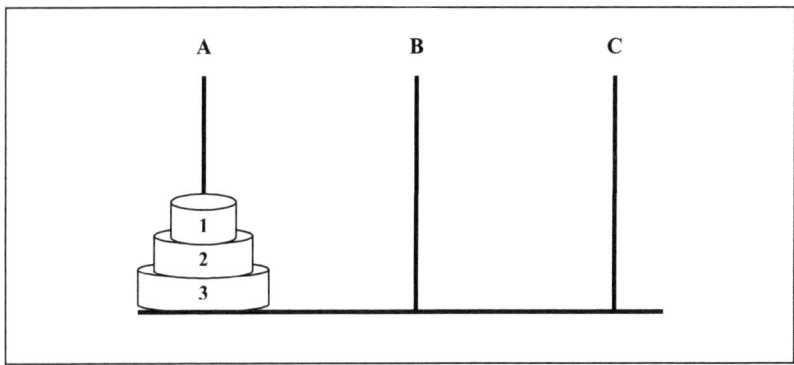

Fig (10) Tower of Hanoi puzzle

The smaller disk takes the ID disk 1, the next one the ID disk 2, and the larger one takes ID disk 3. The idea of the puzzle goes through the following steps:

- Moving disk 1 to tower B and disk 2 to tower C, then move disk 1 from tower B to C.
- Moving disk 3 from A to C, and disk 1 from B to A.
- Moving disk 2 from B to C and disk 1 from A to C.

The transfer of order disks is now completed in tower C and this puzzle can be solved by using java code as shown in List (5) below.

```
class HanoiTwrsApp
{
    static   int   noDisks = 3;
    public   static void main(String[ ] args)
    {
        doTwrs(noDisks, 'A', 'B', 'C');
    }

    public static void doTwrs(int topId, char twrFrom, char inter, char twrTo)
    {
        if (topId==1)
            System.out.println("Disk 1 from " + twrFrom + " to "+ twrTo);
        else
        {
            doTwrs(topId-1, twrFrom, twrTo, inter);        // from---->inter
            System.out.println("Disk " + topId +" from " + twrFrom + " to "+ twrTo);
            doTwrs(topId-1, inter, from, twrTo);        // inter---->to
        }
    }
}                                                      // HanoiTwrsApp end
```

List (5) Hanoi towers puzzle recursive algorithms

6. Conclusion

In computer science the data structures means the way of storing data in a computer memory or disk in a good manner to ensure the efficient use of it. The ease of data retrieval or extraction depends on algorithms. The data structures are directly dependent on the mechanism used to arrange and store the data structure or the type of data structure itself. The benefit of a good design for a data structure is to save time and use less computer memory as possible It is possible to implement a data structure by using any data type or references and any operations or tasks that can be performed on it by using one of the programming languages. Algorithms are the backbone of computer software and the studying of algorithms, in general, is a one of the issues that is very important for any computer programmer, to the extent that we can not find a good program if it is not based on an efficient algorithms. The scope of algorithms is extremely wide, such as compression algorithms, encryption algorithms, search algorithms and sort algorithms

Algorithms that we have studied through this paper describes the general framework to solve problems, whether it's searching, insertion or deletion, but it does not put a specific steps to resolve the problem, and this depends on the programmer understanding of the problem. So perhaps, is a young programmer solves a specific problem in ten steps, while an expert programmer solve the same problem in three or four steps at most. Solving the problem, however, depends on the ability of computer programmer creativity of the solution.

Data structure has evolved with the great development in the technology of computer hardware, and if we take microcomputers as an example, they are developed with a few kilobytes of main memory called registers, then the computer memories expanded to include the RAM and cache memory and also visual memory which is created on fixed disks. The storage media also has evolved from floppy disks with a capacity of 512 KB to fixed disks with large capacities and very high speed. Data structures also followed this evolution and it is evolved form just a small memory variables and sequential files to techniques like the hash tables and a data structures of relational databases.

Extensible Markup Language XML nowadays plays an important role in encoding data in a standard format that is independent of any operating system platform and it support data transfer and data integration. The future development of data structures and algorithms will focuses on java and PHP programming languages as good tools for increasing the productivity of web-based application and manipulates dynamic data structures such as those used in web sites development.

References

1. Allen, Mark. *Data Structures and Algorithm Analysis in java*. 2nd edition (2007). Addison Wesley.

2. Allen, Mark. *Data Structures and Algorithm Analysis in C++.* Third edition (2007). Addison Wesley.

3. Goodrich, Michael. Tamassia, Roberto. *Data Structures and Algorithms in Java.* 4th edition, (2006). John Wiley & Sons, Inc.

4. Goldman, Sally. Goldman, Kenneth. *A practical Guide to Data Structures and Algorithms using java.* (2008). Taylor and Francis group.

5. Harris, Simon. Ross, James. *Beginning Algorithms*. (2006). Wiley Publishing, Inc.

6. Lafore, Robert. *Data Structures & Algorithms in Java*. 2nd edition (2004). Sams Publishing.

7. Skiena, Steven S. *The Algorithm Design Manual.* 2nd edition, (2008). Springer.

8. Abstract data type, http://en.wikipedia.org/.